Yes! <u>You</u> can start your own business

Yes! <u>You</u> can start your own business

No prior experience necessary

David Knight

A Gem from Executive Solution

First published in England 2007
ISBN 978-1-84753-035-6

English edition 2007

In memory of my mentor, best friend
Hero and Dad, John Knight

Who taught me everything and asked for so little

Contents

Our Business is your Business

www.TheExecutiveSolution.co.uk

Acknowledgements

Many people have contributed to the writing of **Yes! You can start your own business**. I appreciate the thousands of loyal customers, clients, suppliers, colleagues, friends and family members that have helped me on my journey whilst writing this book. Their participation in my life over the last decade made possible the discoveries written within these pages.

I am particularly grateful to my wife, Elizabeth, whose support, friendship and hard work is the bedrock that our happiness and successes lies upon. To my lovely son, Jack, for holding back the urge to eat my laptop whilst Daddy was working. Thanks to Steven and Rachael for their critique and encouragement, which are second to none. I am very proud of all of my family!

Thank you to some of the best coaches in the UK: Karen, Jo, Shaun, Sharon and Simon and of course, Kim Morgan, all of whom are so generous in sharing their immense knowledge.

Thank you to my editor, Angela Hooper, for a great job under such tight deadlines. I look forward to working with you again soon.

Thank you to all of the journalists, celebrities and politicians that have chosen to support this book.

I will also take this opportunity to thank all of my colleagues, past and present.

Finally, a big thank you a bit closer to home. Thank you for buying this book. I am certain that you will find this book both enjoyable and informative and would love to hear any feedback you have after reading **YES! YOU CAN START YOUR OWN BUSINESS**

As a reader of this book, you are entitled to sign up to our FREE VIP newsletter via our website . Once you have signed up, I will have the pleasure of being in touch with you and providing you with updates and special offers from The Executive Solution as well as sending you a FREE e-book worth £16.49.

Sign up at www.TheExecutiveSolution.co.uk

You should also check out the Yes! You can start your own business event that is taking place around the UK which compliments this book. The one day training event has received massive feedback as well as lots of media coverage. More information is available via my website above.

I would love to hear from you

You can contact me via

Email
feedback@theexecutivesolution.co.uk

Write

The Executive Solution
2nd Floor
145 – 157 St John Street
London
EC1V 4PY

Introduction

It was just your average Friday evening. I settled down for dinner with my wife and son and talked through the working week that had just passed as we sat there making plans for the coming weekend. Just as we were about to tuck into our roast dinner, the phone rang. It was a family friend phoning up for a bit of 'coaching'.
The conversation that followed went like this:

"I'm going to leave my job and I want to start up my own business."

"Great," I replied, "what's the business going to be?"

"Oh I don't know. I was hoping you could tell me that."

The conversation obviously continued, but I will fast-forward the story up to the point where I sat back down to finish my dinner.
I recalled to Elizabeth, "He was the third person today to ask my advice in starting up a business." That was the point right there in my dining room on a Friday evening where the idea was born to create and write this book. The rest, as they say, is history.

The truth is that starting your own business isn't a perk for a select few. It's something that is **within your grasp**.

Now, the one thing that jumps out at me and seems so consistent when people talk about wanting to own their own business or be their own boss is the wanting of approval, or taking it one step further, it almost it seems they want to be given permission by somebody, to tell them that it is okay to proceed.
Yes! You can start your own business.

Now let me start off with some home truths. **You are amazing** and already have all the potential you need to be successful.

The question is do you know how to **tap in to your amazing inner potential**? Do you even want to?

The fact that you are reading this book indicates that you are taking starting up your own business seriously and by the time you have finished reading **Yes! You can start your own business,** you will be confident in being able to make an informed decision and take those first exciting steps on the road to being your own boss.

Managing your own business can be one of the most rewarding things that you can ever do, but it would be wise to make it clear from the very beginning that it is very hard work and very time intensive, especially at the beginning. It is worth asking yourself the following questions before you begin this journey:

- Can you work hard with self-discipline and under no supervision?
- Can you sell? Can you negotiate?
- Do you believe in yourself and your idea even when other people doubt you?

Okay, so you have answered yes to the questions in the introduction. Great, well let's get cracking then. There are lots of topics to cover....

Here is a health warning…

In NLP (Neuro Linguistic Programming) *See page 82,* it is taught that every individual person has their own map of the world so therefore it is important to remember that everyone is different, and therefore everybody has their own definition of what success means to them.

This book's objective is not to make you conform to a set of rules or guidelines in order for you to start your business. There's no 'magic formula' or 'get rich quick scheme' here. This book is simply a one-way guide based on the experience and research of a group of entrepreneurs. You do not have to follow all of the guidelines laid out before you within **Yes! You can start your own business.** In fact. I urge you not to because the beauty of starting your own business is being able to **be your own boss** and starting off with a blank piece of canvass.

That is the great thing. You can take away from this book what you love and leave behind what you don't care for too much and that will be absolutely the right thing for you and your new business. This is about doing it your way.

Yes! You can start your own business is designed to be a stimulus to help provoke your own ideas and help give you the confidence in knowing that **you are amazing** and that **you can be successful**. There are no guarantees in business, so be careful as to what you are investing in terms of both finance and time and, finally, **have Fun**. Starting a business will be one of the most exciting, rewarding and challenging things you have ever done.

Enjoy it!

"Live as if you were to die tomorrow. Learn as if you were to live forever"

- Mahatma Gandhi -

Fail to prepare, Prepare to fail

Benjamin Franklin

Research tells us that the one thing that new businesses share in common all over the planet is enthusiasm. Great!

All you need to do now is channel that enthusiasm into research. Research is king when starting off. You will need to research suppliers, locations, websites, tax, company formation, bank accounts, copyright; look into what the competition is doing, etc. The list goes on and is huge, and would benefit from you drawing up a list on the next page and then prioritising as to what needs to be researched first. Every business would have a bespoke list, but we have started you off with some generic ideas below as a guide.

Area to be researched	Resource	Priority scale (1/10)
Company Formation	www.companieshouse.gov.uk	
Tax	www.inlandrevenue.gov.uk 08459 154 515	
Business support	www.businesslink.gov.uk 0845 600 9006	

Area to be researched	Resource	Priority scale (1/10)

18

Back to Base'ics
(Not a typo, just the author being clever)

You're going to need a base. Somewhere to work!

A lot of businesses start up from home, often turning a spare room, the loft or even the shed into an office, which may be a good way for your new business to avoid potentially expensive rent. The downside to this is the fact that it can be extremely hard to separate home from work with the office phone always within earshot or being able to see when an email drops in.

A good way of separating the two would be to have set hours just like you would have if working for a company, and try to shut the door on the office. Switch the phone onto voice mail and an out of office on your email. After all, do you really expect other businesses to reply to your calls/emails in the middle of the night?

> A very successful entrepreneur friend of mine, who is based at home, on occasions, actually goes for a walk around the block before returning home and straight into the office to help separate the two.

It is worth noting that there may be tax deductibles by having an office at home and may be possible to claim back from the Inland Revenue a percentage of your home bills e.g. phone, electricity, gas. It is recommended that you speak to an accountant or call the tax office on 08459 154 515 for more information.

If it's not possible to dedicate a whole room in your house as an office, then at least try to dedicate a table or corner somewhere that is only used for your business. For those of you familiar with NLP, this familiar location will soon act as an anchor for you and will help you get into work mode quicker.

You don't need to have an executive style desk with a great big leather chair in your front room. Use whatever works for you. It is reported that Jeff Bezos, founder of the biggest online bookstore Amazon, built his first ever desk out of a door, which was reportedly then bought back by his mother via an online charity auction in 1999 for $30,100.

The moral of the story here is to do what works for you, after all, you are the boss now!

> If you're working from home, do not under-estimate the value of dressing as if you were travelling into work. This will make you feel more professional and will come across to your customers when talking to them over the phone. The opposite is also true if speaking to your customers in your pyjamas.

You may need to consider if you are comfortable with customers coming to your home to discuss business or to pick up their products. If not, a great alternative would be to meet over a coffee in Starbucks or for a more professional approach, you could book a virtual office or meeting room. This can generate a fantastic perception for your company and can cost as little as £9 per hour with no contracts to sign.

There are literally hundreds of companies offering this service on the Internet. Try going onto a search engine and typing in your area followed by virtual office e.g. London virtual office.

www.regus.co.uk
0870 880 8484

www.office-planet.net
0800 085 8326

It is also possible to have postal mail forwarded to your home address or a phone answering service from the above companies. I don't need to tell you that this is a great way to give the perception that you are an established company with a prestigious city address or city phone number, which gives your company a touch of kudos. This address and phone number can then be added to any letterheads, compliment slips or business cards again giving the perception that your business is bigger than it is, thus giving your customer more confidence in your business.

Perception will be crucial as you begin to go to market as customers and suppliers may well be a little bit more hesitant if you give the impression that they are your first ever customer. Have a think about what image you would like your business to have from the customer's point of view and then make a plan in how you can action it.

> You can order business phone numbers (0800, 0870) from the below site
> www.bt.com

It may be worth considering buying a memorable phone number, also known as a golden number, these can cost from £50 and may be a shrewd investment.

Now that you have got your desk sorted out, you will need to populate it with some essential stationery items. Stationery can be bought in high street shops, but could also be worth having a shop around online with the websites below often offering good value for money.

We have provided a useful checklist at the back of the book.

Research

www.ebay.co.uk

www.staples.co.uk
0800 6 92 92 92

www.rymans.co.uk
0800 801 901

> Some ebay.co.uk auctions have a best offer option, which allows you to negotiate a price with the seller. Have a practice now and get good at negotiating. This will benefit you long term when you're negotiating potentially big contracts later on with your business.

So things are coming on nicely, but this desk of yours looks like it might be missing something. Ah that's it, do you need a computer (PC)?

A PC would be a massive advantage at this stage, but don't be overly concerned if you don't have one or cannot afford one just yet. However, I would suggest having one pretty high up on your wish list for the near future.

If you are going to get one, then don't worry about spending loads on one that is capable of playing all the latest games and DVDs, as you will be paying £££s for the graphics and sound card that come with the PC, and besides, you probably wont have time for playing games for a while any way.

When buying a PC, look out for the following options and you won't go far wrong. Also consider if it would be worth opting for a laptop rather then a desktop to give you a bit more mobility and allow you to work from anywhere.

Item	√
Hard drive with capacity to save all your files	
Word processing package (Microsoft Word or similar)	
Monitor for desktops	
Internal modem for Internet	
Fast processor to run large applications simultaneously	
Inkjet printer	
USB drives x 3 + would be great	
CD writer	
Keyboard & mouse	
Anti-virus software	
Digital camera if needing to take pictures for website	

As a guide, £500 should buy you a suitable PC. Be aware that some shops will go for the hard sell when selling extended warranties. It's not for me to say whether this would be good for you and your business, but it might be a good time to practice your new negotiating skills again.

Research	www.dell.co.uk
	www.hp.co.uk

An alternative to buying a computer may be to borrow one from a friend or family member. You can also look into seeing what facilities are provided in your local area, as you may be able to use a PC at your local library for free or perhaps go to an Internet style café to begin with to **carry out your crucial research**.

If you are planning on having a web presence via having a business website, then it would be a wise investment to purchase broadband as this will pay for itself in terms of how much time it will save you as opposed to a dial up internet service provider (ISP).

Below are some broadband suppliers that provide high-speed Internet access from £8.99 per month

Research

www.bt.com
www.aol.co.uk
www.orange.co.uk

If you are going to be highly mobile, but need to keep tabs on your email, then a blackberry might be ideal for you as your email will be sent straight down your mobile phone blackberry handset. Alternatively, there are some very successful entrepreneurs that manage their business solely through their blackberry without the need for a PC.

You can buy a handset from £90 and expect to pay around £20 a month for the service.

www.tmobile.co.uk
www.blackberry.co.uk

It would be impossible to cover off all of the individual tools that you may need for your specific business here e.g. a gardener needing a lawnmower, a rake etc.

Take a few moments and begin to make a list of the essential tools you will need for your business.

Business essentials shopping list

Item	√

What does success look like to you?

I mentioned earlier in chapter one that NLP teaches us that everybody has a different map of the world, or to be put in a different way, everybody has a different perception on life and the things that come with it.

A good exercise that you can try out with your friends and family to illustrate this point is to write down a list of five things, these can be famous people, well known brands, products or maybe a food type, then gather a group of six to eight people and ask them to answer in turn a statement of their feelings against each item that you call out. I can guarantee that each person will interpret each thing differently. Some will be great fans and some people may be completely opposed to the item you call out. This is because everybody has a different map of the world, a different perception of life.

So with this in mind, it would be foolish of me to assume what success means to you. I know what success means to me, but that has no importance to you right now.

Think about being successful

Go on, actually visualise what success looks like to you and your business. What will a **successful you** be doing in twelve months, five years, ten years or when you retire?

What will life look, feel, sound or smell like when you are successful?

Allow yourself to fast forward to a time when you are enjoying this success. What do you see? Where will you be?

Who will be with you?
What does your home look like?
What car are you driving?
What is your bank balance?
What do you do to relax?
What do other people think of you?

Allow yourself some time to think over and enjoy the experience of the above thoughts. Really feel what it's like to be you and **be successful**. You are not watching somebody else's success here, **this is your success**. Begin to enjoy it.

The great news is that you are the director of the movie that you have just been watching inside your head, and you have complete control over all aspects of this movie. You can make the picture bigger and brighter. You can turn the volume up and play it back in surround sound. Over the next few months, allow yourself to have front row seats of this new movie and submerse yourself in what it feels like to be successful time and time again.

A good way of testing your existing life out for size is use the same model. If nothing changes. If you were not to start your own business, what would you be doing in twelve months, five years, ten years etc? Ask the same questions...what will I be doing? Etc.

> *If this type of visualisation is new to you and you're finding this hard, then don't worry. Just keep on practising because soon you will be thinking like a successful entrepreneur and enjoy living and feeling like a success.*

'A goal is nothing more then a dream with a deadline'
Joe L. Griffith

How does it feel to **be in complete control** when you are directing the movie inside your imagination, having complete control over all aspects of what you can see and hear? **It feels great**, right? Of course it does. You are in control. You can see what your definition of success looks like and try it on for size. Now, I'm going to assume that feeling successful is a great feeling for you.

And guess what, Great news! This movie is available to you 24 hours a day, 7 days a week and 365 days a year. Whenever you want to feel successful, just take yourself to that front row seat of your imagination and play back **feeling successful**.

It is worth saying at this point, although not what this book is intended for, that this model works exactly the same way for any feeling that you want to adopt so you can practice replacing successful with happy, confident, sociable, etc.

Whilst you're **feeling good,** this would be a great time for you to write down some goals for your business.

Research shows that only 3% of people write down their goals. Guess what type of people make up the 3% mentioned?
Yes that's right, successful people. **Successful People like you**! Entrepreneurs, business owners and senior leaders

Neuro studies have shown that human beings do not take action until we have imagined taking action through our imagination, and therefore analysing all of the potential risks and keeping ourselves safe. With this in mind, how do you intend to be successful if you cannot imagine being successful. The answer is you won't, so start imagining!

A lot of people that start off their own businesses that turn out not to be successful are the type of people that don't write down their goals, they don't **practice feeling successful**. They do not design and plan their journey, preferring instead, to stumble through their journey.

Think about it. Would you get in the car about to undertake the biggest, most challenging journey of your life and not bother consulting a map, or even worse then that, not even know where the destination (goal) is?

No. Good, I didn't think so.

Think about getting some support via networking…

Great, Ok now would be a good time to start thinking about getting some local support from one of the business support agencies set up in the UK. Their role is to support and assist new businesses, and they would be a valuable phone call at this point as they can assist and offer advice for free of charge on a host of topics from tax to health and safety.

Get them on board early as the chances are they will have knowledge and experience of your desired market place, and could also be able to share some best practice with you that could help you avoid making some mistakes that similar business have made when starting off.

www.businesslink.gov.uk
0845 6009006

Another great way to learn from other people's mistakes and share best practice would be to do a search on the Internet and see if there are any specialist forums for people like you, for example, there may be a bakers forum where bakers can go and leave messages and share ideas, recipes, supplier information etc.

Try it, go onto a search engine and type in your type of business followed by forum e.g. Bakers forum.

www.google.co.uk
www.yahoo.co.uk

Also, don't underestimate the value of talking to people about your idea. A common misconception within new business owners is the fear that people will steal your idea and get to market first. This can make it really difficult to get vital feedback from your potential customers, and therefore very difficult to ensure that you are delivering something that is fit for its purpose. It would be worth bearing in mind that what separates you from most people at this stage are that most people would like to be their own boss and that's brilliant. You are one of the few people who take the next step and put their plan into action.

Whilst you need to be cautious as to whom you are talking to, friends and family can often be a great sounding board to help you talk your ideas through.

It is also worth pointing out here that sometimes people might give you feedback that you might not agree with. These could potentially be golden nuggets, so try not to be too dismissive of feedback, even if it does sound like a hidden criticism. Learn to cherish feedback, do not take it personally. Listen to the feedback, analyze it, try it on for size, if it works, then great, incorporate it and make your business even better. If the feedback doesn't work, then say thank you and keep going!

Also, the last item for this chapter is to research the competition meticulously.

- Find out what they offer.
- How much they charge / special offers.
- How quickly they can deliver.
- Who their biggest clients are.
- Who they target their marketing on.
- Research their advertising, website, retail premises,
- Are they making a profit?

What are you going to do better than your competition?

What will it take for their customers to come to you?

Below is a box to allow you to make some notes on what you can do better then your competition. Don't skip this, it is important!

What do my customers want?
What does my competition do?
What can my business do?

Are you delivering what your customers want?

If not, it might be worth reviewing and tinkering with your plan now.

So what is going to get the money coming in?

Time to get creative

It would be fair to say that one of the biggest decisions you will need to make when starting up your own business is the decision of what you are going to sell.

At this stage, you probably have two options to consider; these are either products or services. There is much to be said in favour of both of these, so let's investigate a little bit deeper.

Argument for selling Products
- Potential high profit margins.
- Customers can see what they are buying.
- Various different outlets in marketing product, e.g. Internet, retail, wholesale.
- Easy to research the competition.

Argument against selling Products
- Manufacturing of product.
- Storage of product.
- Products go out of date/fashion.
- Delivery costs of product.
- Cash tied up in stock.
- Risk of product being damaged

Argument for selling Services
- You and your staff's skill or knowledge is your business.
- Potentially low costs start up if skills already exist.

Argument against selling Services

- Your staff can have ££££s invested in their development and then walk away to work for your competition.

Of course, we are only scratching the surface with the above pros and cons, but allow yourself some time to consider what the benefits and potential risks may be for you and your new business.

Ok, Done that.

Good. So let us review what you have done so far

- Agreed that this is the right time for you to start your new business.
- Reviewed your start up logistics.
- You have set yourself some goals.
- Experienced what success will look and feel like.
- Surveyed the competition.
- Decided on service vs. product or both.

Before we move on.

Ok, I want you to be really honest now. Have you skimmed over the last thirty or so pages just so you can jump into the action pages?

If you have. then I recognise your entrepreneurial 'I want it now' attitude. I can remember when I started my first business, I was so excited to go and meet my customers and sell my products that I skipped over the planning stage as it all seemed a bit dull. I am expecting that some of you share this quality, just like me.

You're probably a person with lots of ideas, lots of energy, but lack patience and just want to get out there and make money. If you have skipped through the last few pages, then I urge you to go back and invest some quality time in laying down some foundations for your new future or you will end up going in completely the wrong direction. Your business will be driving you rather then you driving the business.

Think about it. How huge a part potentially is your new business going to feature in your life?

I am imagining quite a large part.

Would you build your new house without putting down the correct foundations or without researching the local area, or even ensuring that you have all the correct legal documentation in place before steaming straight in and beginning to lay the bricks?

If you have already completed the previous chapters, congratulations! You're one step closer to starting your own business.

The Current Reality

Now, we need to understand where you are now in your life ranging from finance, knowledge, your existing network (contacts) and time.

The above are going to be very important in starting your business.

Finance

Before we talk about money, it is important to highlight right now that you do not need to be a millionaire to start your own business.

It would be easier to start a business if you were wealthy as you would be able to spend a large amount of money on big advertising and modern offices and hire the best staff, but even then, if you don't get the basics right, the business will fail. However much is spent.

Non-wealthy entrepreneurs often start business with very little money of their own. Duncan Bannatyne, who is a prolific entrepreneur and is reported to be worth an estimated £100 million and probably most famous for his role on Dragons den, has gone on record as saying, 'When I started up my first business, all I had in the world was determination and a yellow pages.'

It is also worth noting that he was not an apprentice of a successful tycoon or born into a family blessed with a millionaire's lifestyle. Duncan Bannatyne started off his business empire by selling ice cream. He has gone on record as saying, 'Anybody can do it.'

One of the unspoken presuppositions and key beliefs of entrepreneurs is that money will follow.

Get your idea right, get your timing right, get passionate and work hard and the money will follow.

Ok, so let us review how you are doing financially right now. This is a crucial activity to do now because if you don't have a handle on your current financial position now, then you may run into financial difficulties later on.

Get a copy of your most recent bank statements, credit card statements, household bills, investment details and details of any other income or expenditure, and spend a few moments in filling in the below worksheet.

<u>Income</u>

SOURCE OF INCOME	VALUE	FREQUENCY
e.g. share dividend	*£400*	*Twice per year*
		Total =

Expenditure

SOURCE OF EXPENCE	COST	FREQUENCY
e.g. mortgage	£750	Monthly
		Total =

38

What's the result? (Read as appropriate)

I'm worse off than I thought!

Ok, the first step should be getting some financial advice!

This does not have to be expensive. Your local citizens advice bureau offers a free of charge service.
The next step should be to review all of your expenses and ask yourself some honest questions. (Cut your cloth accordingly) for example, do you need to be spending £45 per month on your satellite TV package when you could have freeview etc?

Now go through each expense with the view of trying to either eliminate the expense completely, or look at taking out a cheaper option or maybe even shop around for a cheaper supplier.

Review your outgoings, now are they in better shape?

Research

www.nacab.org.uk

www.cccs.co.uk

www.nationaldebtline.co.uk

Many new business owners stay in full or part-time employment until their business has really taken off. Is this an option that you need to consider? It will be worth checking out the terms and conditions of your employment contract as some organisations do not allow their employees to start up their own business whilst working for them and can sue you for losses should you break your terms and conditions.

I'm OK, but not rich!

That's fine. It would be wise to keep an eye on your expenditure, and may be beneficial to follow the steps in trying to reduce your outgoings as per above.

How much will you need to earn from the business if you give up your full or part-time job?

It would be really wise to try and save as much money as possible now so that you will have some savings later, should your business have a slow start or hit a seasonal slow period. Business might be slow for you, but I can guarantee that the bank will still want their mortgage payments, etc.

Cut back on the non-essentials. Not only is it an effective state of mind to inherit , but also every penny you save may come in handy at a later date.

I'm Rich!

Great, that should make some aspects of your journey easier and open up a few more options in the way of initially setting up, but you still have a lot of hard work ahead so keep focused!

Knowledge

What do you know that is going to be useful in starting up your own business?

What do you know about your competition?

What do you know about your product/supplier?

What transferable skills do you have from previous work experience or hobbies?

What do your customers know about you or your market place?

If you are selling a service, for example, is there a qualification that you need?

How qualified are other business within your market place?

Network

How many times have you heard the saying, 'it's not what you know, but who you know?

Although often used as an excuse, is actually quite true. Your network of contacts are going to play a major role in how successful you are going to be.

Information or knowledge can be very expensive when first starting out if you have to contract somebody in to your business for advice.

Draw up a long list on the next page of all the people that you know who have knowledge that would be useful to you and your new business. These don't have to be close friends. These people on your list can even be friends of friends. People who are accessible to you. They don't even need to be business experts. One specific skill or piece of knowledge or experience should be enough for you to have them written down on your list.

There are two columns below, one for your contact's name and the second column for you to add any skills or knowledge that they have.

CONTACT NAME	SKILLS OR KNOWLEDGE
For example David Knight www.TheExecutiveSolution.co.uk	Business start up *Could ask him to recommend business banking and company formation advice*

CONTACT NAME	SKILLS OR KNOWLEDGE

If you have more contacts than the grid will allow, then superb. Continue writing down your contacts on a blank piece of paper and be sure to staple it to this page for safekeeping as these will be priceless in going forward for your business.

Take a look at your list of skills/knowledge, have you got all the areas covered off that you would like covered off?

If not, ask your friends and family members if they know of anyone with the specific skill or piece of experience that you are looking for. The key is making your network work hard for you and tap into as much of its depth as possible.

When you think that you have searched your mind for every possible contact on the face of planet Earth, then dip back in and have one last think as this is often the time when you may be pleasantly surprised and have an 'oh yeah' moment.

The secret to networking is to always be on the look-out for new contacts to add to your contact network chart. Start getting out and talking to people. Don't stick with your usual crowd of friends, try talking to new groups of people and practice going around talking to as many people as possible.

A few networking tips below:

1. Have an elevator speech ready.

Always have a fully prepared 30-second statement in your mind ready for when you meet new people. By preparing in this way, you will have a strategically planned map of what you want to tell people in a positive way about your new business. People who don't do this often say far too much to potential customers, or often tell their new public about things that they cannot do.

Plan, be positive and be prepared!

2. Get really good at asking questions and then sit back and listen. Resist the urge of jumping in and finishing people's sentences. Steer the conversation about the person or business of whom you are talking to and listen and learn!

3. Always be on the lookout for new opportunities. Do not go anywhere without a pocket full of business cards. Remember, everyone is a potential contact or customer!

4. Remember to smile and be positive. This can act as a magnet for people wanting to come and network with you. The opposite is true for people that sit there and talk negatively about everything.

For those people you would like to contact that seem a little less within reach (Sir Alan Sugar, for example) remember that although there is a good chance that they will be extremely busy, do not be afraid to ask. What is the worst thing that can happen? A no does not come with an invoice for your money.

I know of many extremely successful people that would be willing to mentor willing enthusiastic people, but very rarely get asked!

Now that may well be because their PA is filtering out the requests, but if you are going to make an approach with someone in Sir Alan Sugar's league, for example, then make sure that your request is different to all the others, i.e., don't ask for money and don't ask him to tell you what to do.

Tell him or her what you can offer him and have a go at practicing some of that marketing yourself stuff we have been talking about earlier.

A lot of highflying entrepreneurs have egos just like me and you, so will probably be flattered for your request for advice.

If this isn't ideal for you, then a great alternative is to do some research by reading books, watching DVDs or by listening to audio books about your chosen business subject, or about a successful entrepreneur's journey.

Because I get asked so often to recommend good books I have set up a recommended reading page on my website www.TheExecutiveSolution.co.uk

There are literally thousands to choose from, but I have listed a few of my favourites on the next page, which I have found especially useful or motivational.

Screw it, let's do it (Lessons in life)
Richard Branson
ISBN 9 780753 510995

Change your life in 7 days
Paul McKenna
ISBN 9 780593 050552

Duncan Bannatyne anyone can do it (My Story)
Duncan Bannatyne
ISBN 9 780752 875 637

Start small, finish big
Fred Deluca & John Hayes

Lessons in Mastery
Anthony Robins
(Audio CD)

My advice would be to always listen out for recommendations of a good book or media resource from friends and colleagues, as even after your business has turned into a huge success, you will always be able to improve at something or enjoy a motivating read.

Time

It is true that most new business owners fixate about their cash flow, but much more than money, your biggest challenge will be time, or rather, lack of it.

Finding the time to do everything that needs to be done is a skill in its own right.

It will be useful for you to review everything that currently fills your working week. Just like you did with your financial expenditure, review each item and ask yourself the question, 'do I really need to watch ten hours of TV soaps every week?'
Being shrewd with your time is again a very useful habit to adopt now, and every hour you save will be crucial going forward.

How much time have you wasted in the last week?

What can you do to become more efficient with your time?

Fine-tune your entrepreneurial imagination

If you were to ask most successful entrepreneurs about their imagination and ask them to actually break down their thought process, be prepared to receive a blank stare.

Most successful entrepreneurs that I know do not schedule in to their busy diaries a thinking session or a brainstorming meeting. The truth is that I believe that entrepreneurs do not actually ever fully turn off.

I include myself in this generalisation. Once you have worked your entrepreneurial imagination, it operates just like an athlete's muscle and will begin to seek opportunities in absolutely everything. The fact is there are opportunities everywhere you look. The entrepreneur's brain has almost childlike wonder and roams free, hunting for that next idea.

Just like athletes, some brains will need more practice then others, but once you have exercised your imagination enough, I really believe that your sub-conscious will take control and will become your most faithful of friends, forever seeking your next opportunity. You will instinctively know once you have successfully exercised your new entrepreneurial mindset enough for what's right for you as you will naturally report back on opportunities tens of times per day.

Now, not every idea that you will think off will have the potential to change the world, so you need to become good at filtering in and out what is worth keeping or rejecting.

A notepad could be a very worthwhile investment and my advice would be to write down absolutely every idea, no matter how farfetched your idea might sound, as this will help exercise your imagination. Only then should you begin to prioritise against your ideas and begin to filter in or out what is appropriate for you and your business right now. Note I said prioritise. My advice is don't ever reject any of your ideas, just keep them in your notebook and review them from time to time as they may one day make you a great deal of money should the marketplace or your customers needs change.

If you are not a note taking kind of person, then a PDA or voice recorder will be equally fine. You will just need somewhere to keep a track of all of your great ideas.

Enjoy practicing this as this is what being an entrepreneur is about. Get good at spotting opportunities in what your customers are telling you via their feedback.

You will get free ideas from your customers, friends and family all the time. Listen to their problems or complaints or even recommendations about other businesses and products. What can you do to make your service better by incorporating their feedback and fulfilling their needs.

> Remember, your ideas do not have to be fully planned business models. The idea here is to encourage your imagination to start getting bigger and stronger.

Becoming a natural entrepreneur is like learning to play a new musical instrument. The more you practice, the better you get and the better you get, the more effortless it will become.

Get great at selling and negotiating!

If you have one, take a look at your CV. How good are you at selling yourself?

The reason I ask is there is probably a very good chance that your new business will require your customers to part with their hard earned money in exchange for your products or service.

Think back to the last five products that you bought! What attracted you to purchase these goods? Snazzy packaging, quality, price, value or a great sales person?

Your customers will be asking themselves exactly the same question when they are given the opportunity to buy from your business. Would you buy your product / service?

How would you like to be approached? I'm guessing you don't like people cold calling you at dinner time so don't expect your customers to welcome you in this way either.

We live in a world where there are world-class sales people and on the other side of the spectrum, there are really poor sales people too. This is great news for you as you can learn from each and every transaction you have with a sales person, regardless of whether they are good or bad.

If you experience a bad sales person, **you have just learnt a whole host of techniques** in what not to do with your customers. Alternatively, if you witness a great sales technique, then try that on for size with your new customers.

Also, don't be shy to ask great sales people how they become so good at sales. I am certain that if approached by you in the right way, they will take this as a great compliment and may be willing to pass on some advice or training tips

As with all new skills, if you're not a natural sales person, then try and get some experience on board before dealing with your new customers for your new business.

Remember, every customer that you serve via your new business will go away and provide PR work for free. They will tell everybody if they have received either a really good or really bad experience, so you need to make sure that you are selling well. Not just your products, but your company's brand as well.

> Do not underestimate the power of word of mouth. It is FREE and it is effective advertising.

Remember that everything is negotiable in business. It's an unwritten law. You will need to negotiate with all of your suppliers to get the best deal so do not be offended when your customers try and negotiate with you.

Negotiation is not exclusive to price. Negotiation is about getting the best possible product / service for the best possible price. It is about value.

Remember, people like to save money. There are quite a few high street shops that have made millions of pounds from having an almost permanent 'closing down 80% off, everything must go Sale'.

Their customers' perception is that they have got a real bargain. The fact that their RRP price was an 'untruth', shall we say, is irrelevant. People like saving money and the real clever piece of marketing behind this is people also like scarcity, so a closing down sale ticks both the boxes.

Genius? I'll let you be the judge.

There will be plenty of opportunities for you to sharpen up your negotiation skills over the coming weeks. Be aware it might feel a bit uncomfortable at first, but you will soon become an expert negotiator with a little bit of practice.

> Not negotiating does not bear thinking about. I can guarantee that your competitors will negotiate from your suppliers, so will therefore be receiving your products at a cheaper price. So straight away before you even start, your competition would have the capacity to under price you and potentially put you out of business before you have even begun.

The harder you negotiate, the cheaper you can potentially deliver your product for. There are lots of factors into negotiating well. The more you buy, as an example, would normally indicate a bigger saving as you are buying in bulk, but then you hold the risk of not being able to sell all of your products. So have a good think about what your negotiation strategy should be for your business.

If you are thinking of starting a service business, do not just skim over these works assuming that negotiating does not concern you. I have a very good friend who runs a coaching business and deals with many large blue chip companies across Europe and he regularly tells me of his negotiation stories. His customers often negotiate on price and service bundles. It is business, after all.

Remember when negotiating:

If you don't ask, you don't get.

Also, remember that the more your customer has gone away from the transaction feeling that they have negotiated a good deal, the happier a customer you will have. If either of you walk away from the business transaction feeling like you have been squeezed too hard, then you both lose out. You won't be doing business with that person again. Try to ensure that everybody is happy in every deal you do.

Try practicing negotiation at every opportunity from now on. Always try and get something thrown into the deal as a bonus or something off of the price of anything you buy.

Selling and negotiating might come naturally to you, but if not, remember not to give up. This is the key difference between successful entrepreneurs and those that do not make it in the world of business.

Try hard to develop a thick skin now as the chances are you will experience numerous challenges whilst starting your business, and at times, you might feel that the world is against you. Be positive and just get back on that horse again and keep trying.

When Thomas Edison was questioned over his failed attempts at creating the light bulb, he replied, 'I have not failed. Not once, I have simply found many different ways in how a light bulb cannot work.'

In fact, Thomas Edison has left behind a catalogue of fantastic quotes that may be useful to take a look at now:

> The three great essentials to achieve anything worthwhile are, first, hard work; second, stick-to-itiveness; third, common sense.

> The successful person makes a habit of doing what the failing person doesn't like to do.

> Genius is 1% inspiration and 99% perspiration. Accordingly, a genius is often merely a talented person who has done all of his or her homework.

> Opportunity is missed by most people because it is dressed in overalls and looks like work.

What's in a Name?

You may already have a name in mind for your new business. Or if you haven't, now would be a good time to start thinking about it. What would you like your company to be called?

Some people think this is very important to have a really good company name. I have known others who have delegated the job of naming their company to other people such as family members or friends. I also know of one person that named their business after their car registration plate, hence making her number plate personalised!

The truth is today it is worth spending a little bit of time considering what you want to get across to your customer via your company name. Today, there are many things to consider such as how much the domain name for your company might cost (web site address) or even is it still available.

Below are a few guiding points for you to consider before settling on a name.

1. A name that describes what your company is about can be useful such as Spec Savers, Easy jet, Blockbusters, Kwik-fit. Although, consider also that this can be limiting if you plan on having a huge business empire long term that will develop your portfolio of products or services.

2. Your family name could help give the perception of a personal touch, but can also give the impression that you are a small company, although companies such as Marks and Spencer's, J Sainsbury's, Ford Motor Company and WH Smith do counter-argue the point.

Would giving your customers the feel of a personal touch benefit your company?

A well-known TV entrepreneur recently said that he would normally always opt for a company that uses a family name when contracting in service people, as he feels that anyone that uses their name against their products or service will have to be pretty sure of themselves.

3. Is location an important factor for your business? Are you hoping for local loyal support and custom? Are the products you're selling coming from a certain place? For example, Cornish pasties. If so, consider using the town name, but again, be careful of the consequences of having the perception of being small.

Spend a bit of time brainstorming lots of names and trying on different names for size, but do remember that although a good company name can be an asset if the rest of your business is in good working order, then your company name should not be a showstopper. Companies like IKEA and ESSO are good examples of this, in my opinion.

Once you have settled on a name, just before you go and get your business cards printed out, take a look on the companies house website and just make sure that somebody has not beaten you to it. It may also be worth checking out the trademark website too.

www.companieshouse.gov.uk

www.uktrademarkregistration.com

Once you have the green light and have settled on a name, ask some friends and family what they think of when you tell them your company name.

Then review their feedback against your original objectives. If you're happy that it is consistent with what you're looking to pitch, then you now have a company name.

Congratulations!

Putting together A Business plan

Despite what you may have read in other books, a Business plan is not just a tick in the box to get a bank to lend you lots of money.

In fact, A sound business plan will be a very useful tool to you and your business and will be worth its weight in gold over the coming months. A well-structured plan will help you realise when you are making good against your promises to your customers, it will help you know when to **celebrate your business success**, but most importantly, it will help lay those solid foundations that we spoke about earlier on in the book.

There will be people out there that will offer to write your business plan for you, which will come with guaranties of 'the bank will love this'. Do not be tempted.

Who needs to understand every word and every proposed figure in their business plan? You do. You will be the person responsible for action against this plan and making good of all of your objectives that you have set out in the hope of turning your dream into a success. Your business plan will need to be consulted on a regular basis in the early days so you might as well learn to love it now.

Besides, how are you going to answer the bank managers' questions when they wish to explore some of your figures?

So what is a Business plan? A business plan is a plan that works for a business in planning a way forward, allocate resources, focus on business specific criteria and help prepare for potential problems and opportunities.

Just in case you're becoming a bit worried now, don't be. The truth is that if you have been completing the activities set out within this book, then you have already started to form your business plan without realising. See, it is not so hard, is it? There are lots of books available specifically aimed at helping you write a really good business plan and I fully recommend that you invest in one or two as a useful reference, but we will aim to cover off the basics now by giving you a whistle stop overview in how to write a business plan.

You might also want to research a computer programme called Business plan pro.

www.bplans.com

SECTION ONE

Section one should be an Executive Summary providing an overview of your business plan and pointing out highlights and opportunities. The objective of the Executive Summary is to give the reader enough information on your business without having to read the whole plan in great detail.

Items to consider

- The turnover in the first year will be (£??)
- The profit/Loss in the first year will be (£??)
- The business will begin to make profit once sales of (£??) have been achieved. This is expected to be achieved in (Date??)

SECTION ONE (A)

Provide a brief company description with details of any legal establishment, history, milestone dates of start up etc.

SECTION TWO

Section two should be dedicated to planning who your customers are. Typically, this section will span two pages and will talk about every different type of customer with whom you plan to serve.

You will need to distinguish between Business Customers and consumer customers and detail what their needs are and write how you plan to meet these.

It would be wise to have researched and supplied information on how your competition is doing and how they serve their customer, and highlight how you propose to be better than them at fulfilling their customers' needs.

Then describe in detail how many potential customers you have, and outline where they are and plan how you are going to reach these customers. Outline who they shop with now and how much they spend and even how they choose to pay.

If it is possible, it may even prove useful for you to identify specific large customers that you have within your radar and even more importantly, identify how much of a budget they have for your products or service.

If at this point you can have some sort of commitment or feedback on your proposal from your potential customers that they will be looking to shop with you, top marks!

SECTION TWO (A)

Describe what you are selling. Whether it is a product or service or maybe both. Keep a focus on the customer benefits and give an outline of how much you plan to sell your products for against how much your competition is selling it for.

SECTION THREE

Section three is where you need to sell yourself as an asset to your company along with anybody else who is going to be starting with you. This typically should again be around two pages in length and should be very much tailored around any transferable skills or experience that you have that will benefit your new business.
This is not the place to tell the world that you make great cakes unless you are starting up a rival business to Mr Kipling.

Instead, you want to make sure that this outlines all of you and your team's strengths by giving a short overview of yourself and each member of staff, including career and educational background, work experience and key skills that are transferable to your company.

There will also be a need for you to attach a CV for each of you and your employees, which should be submitted within the appendix of your business plan.

If you don't have a CV or need it updating, then visit my website.
Top class CV's from as little as £65 each
Visit
www.TheExecutiveSolution.co.uk

SECTION FOUR

Section four should be used to outline all of the resources that you both have and will need in the business and why you need them, how you plan to source them and how much they will cost and when you plan to acquire them. Take as much space as needed, as this is important, but try to present it on no more then five pages, ideally.

It may be useful to review the notes you made on Page 25 in writing up your essential shopping list.

Below is also a small list to help you get started.

- Premises / decoration / furniture
- Transport
- Utilities
- Technology (IT, Communications, Software)
- People
- Banking / accountancy
- Business Consultation
- Research

It would also be useful to detail any assets that your business currently owns, should there be any.

Ok, so how are you finding it so far?

Good?

Great, well done, because we're getting through this nicely now.

SECTION FIVE

Section five should be used to outline a report on what suppliers you plan to use. This will include what they will supply you with, why you have chosen this particular supplier and at what price.

Don't forget to highlight here any discounts that you have negotiated thus far.

It would be wise to also provide a list of backup suppliers should you encounter any problems with your first choice.

Not putting all of your eggs in one basket, etc.

SECTION SIX

This section is all about the competition to your business. Reviewing your work from Page 34 would be very useful at this stage.

Things to ensure that are covered:

- Who is your greatest competition in the market place?
- Who are your local rivals?
- How will you be compared to your competition?
- Why are customers going to buy from you rather then your rival?
- Why are customers going to buy from your rival rather then you?
- What does your competition do well?
- What can you do better then your competition?

SECTION SEVEN

This is where you will need to detail your financial plan. Things to include here are profit and loss, cash flow forecast, balance sheet, break-even analysis, assumptions, business ratios, etc. Some of this may seem quite difficult first time round, so make sure you are making full use of your network including business link, and seek financial advice from a qualified accountant.

Let's cover this in a little more detail on the next page

Cash Flow

The amount of cash earned after paying all expenses and taxes. The actual movement of cash. Cash inflow minus cash outflow.

Balance Sheet

Also known as the statement of financial condition. The balance sheet is a quantitative summary of your company's financial position, which includes assets, liabilities and net worth.

Break-Even Analysis

The break-even point for a product is the point where total revenue received equals total costs. A break-even date is typically calculated in order to determine your business financial risk

Assumptions

Here is where you will detail any assumptions that are used as the justification of the financial figures that you have outlined within your business plan.

SECTION EIGHT

The final section, section eight is where you need to detail your contingency plans against potential problems that may occur, and illustrate how you would plan to tackle such problems. This is a crucial part of your business plan as this is where you will supply evidence on how versatile and dynamic you and your business can be.

You will need to supply details to show that you are prepared for a diverse and wide range of possibilities, and that your business under your leadership can take these varying possibilities in your stride.

Below is a list to get you started in what you might want to factor in:

Environmental changes

How will changes in the climate affect your customers or your business? Will your customers' buying habits change? Are you insured against weather damage?

Political changes

What law changes could affect your business? Would a change in government cause a change in your business?

Culture changes

Can your business become unfashionable? Are you starting up a passing fad company? Will the next latest craze affect your sales? What is the public's opinion of your marketplace?

Developmental changes

Can your business be affected by changes in technology? Will your customers' opinions of your business change based on generational changes?

Marketplace changes

What can your competition do to affect your business?

- Start a price war
- Release a better product/service
- Spend big on advertising
- Target your business or customers

You will need to illustrate that you have researched into your customers' buying habits.

Does your customer spend more money in your marketplace at a certain time of the year? If you are selling Christmas trees, then I would guess so. Therefore, what will your business be selling during the summer months?

What will you do if your suppliers go bust?

Begin to think about how you would tackle such changes and factor in a contingency plan against each risk.

This section should take up about three pages and the more research and time that is invested into this section, the more future proof your new business will become.

The rule of thumb here is by planning for every eventuality, you will have more chance of being able to ride through any difficult times.

Review

Okay, well done. You have just formed your very first business plan. That wasn't so bad, was it?

Like with all things, feedback can be crucial so give your new business plan a test drive and show a few close friends or partners and see how easy to read it is.

Your aim here is for your business plan to be self-explanatory without the need for you to offer a commentary to explain vague areas.

Roles and Responsibilities

By now, I am certain that you would have had a good think about who you would like working in your business.

When you were reading the book right at the beginning visualising what success looked like to you and your business, were there groups of people working away under your control or were you a one person band juggling all of your business responsibilities on your own?

If you are planning to manage the business completely on your own, then this section will be easy for you, as you will have to do everything.

However, if your new business centres on involving other people, then if you haven't already, you will need to begin to decide who you want working alongside you.

Now this will arguably be one of your biggest decisions as your team can help make or break your new business, so place careful consideration into what skills and behaviours would benefit your business. It may not be enough to offer someone a job just because they are related, a friend, kind, cheap or good-looking. (However tempting that may be.)

It would be extremely valuable for you to jot down all of the essential skills that are needed for your business to be a success and then tick off what skills you already possess within yourself on the grid supplied on the following page.

Any skills that are not currently held within your business will help form your job specification for any potential new employees joining your new business

Essential skills required

Skill	Tick
Entrepreneurship	

Okay, so first question, do you know anybody that can fill the above skill requirements?

Do you know anything about their work ethic or attitude?

Can you see yourself working alongside this person?

I have heard in the past both good and bad stories from people starting up a business with friends or relatives.

Let me take this opportunity and talk a little bit about different levels of relationship tolerance.

Here is an example; consider the friend that you have known socially for years. The kind of friend that you would meet up with once a month and have a good catch up with over a drink or two.

Have you ever been on holiday with this friend? Does the friendship begin to come under a little bit of strain after four or five days of compromising over which restaurants or bars you should go to?

Okay, let's crank it up a bit. Have you ever lived as flat mates with this friend? Have you had to endure your friend's unusual habits and unsociable demands?

Well, the reason I ask is going into business with a friend or family member is a bit like the next level up from living with them. At times, there will be no escaping the pressures and demands of your customers or suppliers.

Would you feel confident in raising potential performance issues or a bad attendance record with a friend who is working within your business?

How would your friend or family member feel about you being their boss and, at times, having to carry out your orders?

Also, consider the rationale behind you going into business with somebody else.

I have met many people who when questioned as to why they chose their business partner or employees have said that it was more down to circumstance; e.g. that person being out of work, rather then the person fulfilling a specific skill shortage.

I have also met many people that chose to go into business with a partner because that way they feel that they have a ready made safety net should anything go wrong.

It wasn't my fault, it was theirs.

You don't need me to tell you that if you are considering starting up with someone else just for their company so you don't get lonely, or as above, an excuse should things go wrong, then this is potentially a very expensive decision.

However, if this person is filling a skill gap or is an asset, then great, this could be both great fun and very successful.

My last tip here is to be really specific when deciding on who does what role, otherwise it will lead to a lot of confusion and therefore tasks can potentially get overlooked. Have a clear decision making process and don't be afraid for your employees to make decisions specific to their role. This will lead to them being really engaged with your business and becoming really committed to your success. Just be clear upfront about your expectations.

Selling your company to a potential partner/ employee

If you have identified somebody that would be perfect as an employee or partner, then there is a good chance that they may need some reassurance before joining a brand new business.

How do you plan to sell your business to potential employees?

First of all, I recommend doing some digging around to find out how much the typical salary would be for their role within your market place. You know how much you can afford and I strongly suggest cutting your cloth accordingly, even if this means offering somebody a part time role initially.

It could be useful initially to get people to work for your company as contractors. This means that there are less commitments as an employer, and means that lots of the potential time-consuming aspects to employment can be left until you are big enough to hire someone specifically to manage your payroll and employment commitments.

Business Banking

You should now have written up your business plan, which will come in very handy when meeting your new bank manager. It is important to point out that there is a lot of choice available to you as a business customer, so don't feel obliged to sign up with the first bank manager you meet.

Although it might not feel like it, the process of meeting your bank manager during your initial meeting should be a two-way interview. Your role is to outline your business idea and the bank manager's role is to outline how they can help you and sell the bank as the right solution to you also.

Attend the meeting with your bank manager with a set of questions that are important to you.

For example, if you plan on handling a lot of cheques, it will be quite important to find out if there is a limit on how many cheques you can pay in on any given day and also if there is a charge for paying in cheques?

If you plan on asking the bank for money in way of a business loan, then make sure that you are confident in selling yourself as low risk. In my experience, most banks are very cautious in lending brand new businesses money without it being secured against your home, so do not take rejection personally at this stage.

I urge you to seek independent financial advice before borrowing any money as the consequences of not paying your business bills could mean you losing your home.

Getting an accountant

It is commonly said that a good accountant will pay for themselves in what they can help you save by their knowledge of the UK tax law etc. A good accountant can be a great asset to your company by using their experience and contacts to advise and support you in a wide range of subjects. (A good accountant can do a lot more for your company then just prepare your tax bill.)

Your Bank manager (if you have one now) may well have a list of accountants in your area that they can recommend.

Remember when meeting up with potential accountants that you are paying them, so make sure that you are confident in asking them questions that will help you.

Below are a few questions to have in mind.

- Have they any experience in operating accounts for any other similar businesses within your market place?

- Can they help you with company formation?

- Can they help you find the funding you need?

- Can they help you fill in your personal tax return?

- Can they provide examples of helping other small businesses?

- Can they offer you a fixed price quote for their service?

If the thought of all this financial work is making you feel a bit giddy, then don't worry, you are not alone. I know of very few entrepreneurs that enjoy getting stuck into the nuts and bolts of their accounts, and much prefer the sales side of the business. But do not underestimate how important it is to keep an eye on this side of your business.

After all, it is the one clear indicator you have of how successful you're being at business.

Check out the below sites for popular accounts software:

www.quickbooks.co.uk

www.sage.co.uk

Forming a company Structure

We are beginning to get to the stage now where you can consider putting a bottle of your favourite champagne in the fridge on ice in readiness to celebrate the official opening of your new company.

You have one final large decision to make. How are you going to register your business?

- Limited Company
- Sole trader
- Partnership

Now, many of the people you have met (bank manager, accountant, etc.) would or should have discussed this with you already.

It would be impossible to offer you sound advice as to what would be the best option for you and your business in this book, as every business would benefit from various different approaches, so my advice would be to do some serious research and really make your new network of contacts work hard for you.

Below are some recommendations to research:

www.businesslink.gov.uk

www.companieshouse.gov.uk

If you are planning on setting up as a limited company, then the below business can help with the paperwork at a fixed price:

www.uk-plc.net

Registering with the Inland Revenue

If you have not registered with the Inland Revenue, then now is the time to do it.

www.hmrc.gov.uk

Companies Registry on 0845 300 6555

The Inland Revenue are not only there to take a cut of your profits. They can also be very useful in giving you some advice when you are just starting. I recommend giving them a call and arranging a meeting with your local IR business manager.

Registering with other Departments

You may or may not need to register with the following organisations and departments, but I would recommend finding out now just to be sure.

VAT 0845 010 9000

Health & Safety Executive (HSE) 0845 345 0055

Also, dependant on what type of business you have will be dependant on what else you may need to be registered to.

Contact business link and ask for their advice.

www.businesslink.gov.uk

Well, this is my stop and this is where I need to say goodbye and wish you the very best of luck for your new business.

I am sure you will now agree with me that **YES! YOU CAN START YOUR OWN BUSINESS.**

You will be interested to know that there is a nationwide training event tour taking place across the UK to compliment this book. More information at www.YesYouCanStartYourOwnBusiness.com

---

I will leave you with one last piece of advice before I go.

Do not give up,

Remember why you are better than the competition.

Visualise success, be that success and most importantly, have fun!

Until next time,

Good Luck

Useful Websites

Business coaching www.TheExecutiveSolution.co.uk
Advice on start up www.Startups.co.uk
Practical advice www.Buildyourbusiness.co.uk
Practical advice www.MyBusiness.co.uk
Essential viewing www.Businesslink.gov.uk
Entrepreneur website www.Planetentrepreneur.co.uk
HM customs www.HMRC.gov.uk
Companies house www.companieshouse.gov.uk
Business banking www.Barclays.co.uk

Network at breakfast, network anytime - a recommended
approachable, un-stuffy starting point for any business
www.4networking.biz

ARE YOU A COACH OR PSYCHOTHERAPIST

GET VISABILITY IN THE MARKET PLACE

JOIN THE COACHING POOL NOW

Email feedback@TheExecutiveSolution.co.uk

Additional notes and resource

WHAT IS NLP (NEURO LINGUSTIC PROGRAMMING?

Neuro Linguistic Programming was created and developed in the early 70s by Richard Bandler and John Grinder via their studies at the University of California at Santa Cruz. This was no ordinary study, their use of technology from linguistics and information science, combined with insights from behavioural psychology and general systems theory were used to unlock the secrets and magic of highly effective communication.

The creators of NLP were interested in how people influence one another, and in the possibility of being able to duplicate the behaviours and therefore performance of highly effective and influential people.

The methodology and specific NLP technology makes it possible to discover much of what the human brain does that he or she is not aware of.

The word **Neuro** refers to an understanding of the brain and its functioning. **Linguistic** relates to the human communication aspects (verbal and non verbal) and **programming** is the behavioural and thinking patterns processed by the human brain.

For more information on NLP, I recommend:

Neuro Linguistic programming for dummies
Romilla Ready & Kate Burton
ISBN 9 780764 570285

Stationery shopping list

Item	√
Pens	
Pencils	
Pencil sharpener	
Desk tidy for pen storage	
Calculator	
Stapler	
Hole punch	
Scissors	
Ruler	
Tape	
Notice board	
Desk lamp	
Paper clips	
Selection of envelopes	
Diary current and next year	
Wall calendar	
Contact address book	
Sticky tack	
Post it notes	
Ream of white paper	
Note pads	
Ring binders	
Expense book	

DAVID KNIGHT

THE EXECUTIVE SOLUTION
(CEO)

> **Yes! You can start your own business author**

Is one of the UK's most enthusiastic and entertaining speakers on entrepreneurship and motivation in the UK

His dynamic and action packed presentations are both Educational and fun, which leave his audiences feeling inspired, challenged and super charged.

The Yes you can start your own business tour is taking place across the UK in 2007

This one day event is designed for entrepreneurs by entrepreneurs and will bring the learning from this book to life.

Demand is high with limited numbers available so please be sure to book early to avoid missing out!

Visit
www.TheExecutiveSolution.co.uk

This fantastic event will enable you to:

1. Set Clear and accurate goals for your new business
2. Understand The 7 secrets to effective marketing which will save you ££££'s
3. Pitch your business effectively within 60 seconds to potential customers
4. Learn to negotiate and sell effectively (The Lifeline of any business)
5. Understand what your customers want
6. Get to know your marketplace in explicit detail
7. Visualize your success and knowing when you have it
8. Managing your most precious commodity effectively (Your Time)
9. Establish an effective and reliable network so you know who can support you and when
10. How to get the maximum value out of the smallest investments also known as the Millionaires perception (including FREE media coverage)

Not To mention the opportunity to set your own agenda learning points at the beginning of the session which will be covered during the day

There is more

Your tutor for the day will be the fantastic Author of YES! YOU CAN START YOUR OWN BUSINESS David Knight

Information packed Event with the opportunity to bespoke your own objectives

Fantastic Networking Opportunity to meet other Entrepreneurs and business owners

Cherry picked Executive Venues with all inclusive refreshments and Lunch

A Yes You can start your own business certificate

A leather-bound folder and Exclusive pen

Comprehensive guide and hand outs

A 10% discount voucher for any future events or merchandise

Access to the TES forum

Full use of The Executive Solution Entrepreneurs group logo for use on your marketing and website materials

Added as a friend on our famous MYSPACE page

Book NOW at

www.TheExecutiveSolution.co.uk

Look out for

YES! YOU CAN GET THAT JOB

YES! YOU CAN DO PUBLIC SPEAKING

Coming Early 2007

Are you looking for a FREE business forum. A place where you can meet new friends, colleagues and customers

The TES Message board is that place

www.TheExecutiveSolution.co.uk

* * * *

JOIN OUR **VIP** MEMBERS NEWS LETTER

For FREE

www.TheExecutiveSolution.co.uk

Excellent reviews for

Yes! <u>You</u> can start your own business

"I certainly think this will be a valuable guide to business start up and congratulate David Knight on it. It is the aspiration of millions to establish their own companies; to be their own boss; and to have a chance to make serious money. This short, easily read, accessible book is a very practical guide, based on real experience, as to how get started and maximize the chances of success"

Vincent Cable MP Shadow Chancellor of the Exchequer

"Yes! You can start your own business is certainly a useful tool for those setting up a business"

The RT.Hon.Sir Menzies Campbell C.B.E Q.C M.P

"This man means business"

A leading Kent newspaper

THE TES NEWS ROOM

Executive Solutions

The Executive Solution Ltd publishing division are passionate about working with only the best authors and leaders within the world of Business.

If you feel that you have exceptional talent and would like to be considered for a future project then please contact us at feedback@theexecutivesolution.co.uk

Printed in the United States
88599LV00002B/22-30/A

9 781847 530356